FROM THE
ARAPAHO SONGBOOK

FROM THE
ARAPAHO
SONGBOOK

Andrew Schelling

LA ALAMEDA PRESS   ALBUQUERQUE

Some of the poems "From the Arapaho Songbook" have appeared in
Bombay Gin (Naropa University), *ecopoetics* (Jonathan Skinner), *Mandorla*
(Kristin Dykstra & Roberto Tejada), the *Spoon River Review* (Kirsten
Hotelling Zona) and on Jerome Rothenberg's "Poems & Poetics" blog.
Bob and Susan Arnold made two little fold-out books for their
Longhouse series: *from the Arapaho Songbook* and *Arapaho Songbook II*.
A dedication poem, "Shall We Offer Flowers?" that appeared in
Tricycle: The Buddhist Journal contained a dozen lines from this book.
I want to thank the editors & readers of all these publications.
The small press is the natural habitat of the poem.

Cover painting: MOONLIGHT, WOLF, Frederic Remington, 1909
oil on canvas, Addison Gallery of American Art
Phillips Academy, Andover, Massachusetts

Frontispiece: SUNG MOUNTAINS, JB Bryan, *ink on paper*

Schelling, Andrew.
From the Arapaho songbook / Andrew Schelling.
p. cm.
ISBN 978-1-888809-61-9 (alk. paper)
I. Title.
PS3569.C4796F76 2011
811'.54--dc22

2011004235

La Alameda Press
9636 Guadalupe Trail NW
Albuquerque, New Mexico 87114

This book uses words from other languages than American English.
Some are drawn from the Sanskrit, Ute, Spanish, Haida, Hindi, or
Chinese. However most are from Arapaho, an Algonkian tongue.
In almost every case a translation occurs nearby.
There is a glossary of terms at the back of the book,
along with specific notes on the poems.

•

Single Algonkian words are like tiny Imagist poems.
Edward Sapir

nix – onookee
nix – onookee

heet – won – ni'ii – notonee – noo
heet – won –ni'ii – notonee – noo

Out there a lone buffalo
I am going to make medicine with him

Arapaho Ghost Dance song #33

CONTENTS

Protein residue occurs
on 83 knife, flint, & axe edges,
oh the falcons hang
13,000 years
above a smoky blue cache
what animals the tools scraped,
teb-iinis broken horn
wox niiinón bear tepee
but those peaks there, no, never,
'it is never summer there'

White owls
northern bodies
learning all you can about language—
the hammer mountain range
willows, willows
the many things done
with a verb
can you speak one that pierces the heart?
wox noho'kuhnee-t
'where the mule deer sings'

What are the lineages of life?
nótonohein: solar waves
ground water, radiant light
up valley a relict glacier
the bulk of it hidden
listen it's the underlying beat of the watershed
the shapes of earth twist we don't see them
medicinal plants poisons the mints
gather in singular places
at *hooxéb* the mouth of the spring

Bitter buffaloberry
devil's club tangled dogtooth
narrowleaf arrowhead
skyrocket chicory bluestem
few-flowered shooting star
Indian pipe
all the paradise you need's outside your door
one-sided wintergreen self-heal
earth puts forth her medicines
yellow owl's clover prairie smoke

Last I saw
she was reading & destroying them
the suitcase full of letters
the cottonwood song
neniibéit-owoo
I am singing it,
what would she do with them,
songs for all those cottonwoods
I mean a bit of money's
what use to her?

What we call
Sawtooth mountain
'eagle's nest'
Algonkian tongue full of verbs
the old guy's a legend he
left a suitcase of letters
you can't exactly run through
San Francisco
crying they're burning
the letters of Jaime de Angulo

Questions for Mary Fabilli—
When did she meet & how
Jaime de Angulo
Did Bill Everson also visit & was he
asking after Jeffers
Why did LB write that you
introduced Ruth Hallisey and why
after all the revulsion Jaime
showed the Catholic Church did the
church people go
out to find him?

Phoned Fish & Wildlife
disappointment &c
sympathize with the pressure
delisting &c
afraid wholesale slaughter
puzzled that in those
latitudes only nine
ten moons appear
the moon does not appear
one full season above the Arctic Circle
Moon of wolves running

Two brilliant old cranks
the one living in a cage the other
dying of cancer
contemplating the irony
the absurdity
the humor in their
respective fates
cóoó' the trap, so named
because game animals were
driven & trapped there
humor absurdity irony

Tongue river, goose river
place where the water disappears underground
hohokee-no'oowu' crazy house
& the white sandstone rocks where
chiefs got drunk—
then the story about
Catholics hanging
prayer charms him not
knowing to the
side of his hospital bed
crazy house

Caribou horns cast their moss
the leaf turns yellow
the leaf falls
snow falls from the leaves
the late fall moon the severe moon
moon glint on fresh ice
eagle moon bustard moon the budding moon
moon of the rut
moon when animals molt
moon of great departure

Ruth why do you want
to know these things it is all
right to talk about in
a general way, with certain reservations
the necessary care powerful & dangerous
as lightning
Look at the harm raw
psychoanalysts do their
patients the actual details
handling all esoteric knowledge

Time-reckoning
inexact as blossom time,
local & economic conditions predominate
Orion's Belt Ursa Major
the morning & evening stars
from new to full we reckon the moons
with seasonal names
 "There is no case in which
the month term is etymologically
unrelated to that for moon"

For the Chinese too
month character
is as moon character

月   *yue 4*

we who have seen it wander
the bright Hop Alley streets at night
past the former limestone brothel
might there be one among us
who remembers the tribes
from Sonora
to the northern taiga

Thick fog quarter moon
the great dictionary
the thousand lunar journey companion
what is the dark crater
what the *pa-wi-ro-peku*
set into the front of my head antlers
antler research I call it
always on the track of something
PROTECT MEN & CATTLE
oldest three-word poetry prayer

Dear Eck the word rut
is used largely in circles of
hunters & naturalists
most people here dwell at too far a remove
from animal cycles for it to sit
high in the lexical toolkit
belling sounds antiquated too ornamental
more commonly deer call or cry
elk bugle
here our coyote ululate

Wild animal names
are taboo in our mouths
eti-notiih-o'u
I am going to look for it
linguists call it taboo replacement
we say racks instead of antlers
the visitor from up north
eti-neyei-neh'-yei-noo
I am going to try to kill it
deformation is my form of research
thick fog April moon

```
KINNIKINNIK
INNIKINNIKK
NNIKKINNIKI
NIKINNIKKIN
IKINNIKKINN                    bearberry
KINNIKKINNI
INNIKKINNIK
NNIKKINNIKI
NIKKINNIKIN
IKKINNIKINN
KKINNIKINNI
```

Awake in the lodgepole pine forest
red berries a man's dream
down on all fours
call the earth sinewy
violet veins run the root of it
with a morning hard-on to piss, noting
the sap, the *soma*
three basic intimations rise up
moon-words in Sanskrit
three separate moons
into the leathery bearberry

It was the town where my
friend shot himself
along the North Pacific Rim
salmon in creeks deer in the
hills he stopped the car
another friend observes in a poem that
he did not anticipate
plummeting into an abyss
he stressed rational inquiry
western red cedar wild ginger

Thirty years testing the
California notion of luck, *dinihowii*
musicians where the cliff overhangs
toss me the gambling bones
two years asking why did he shoot himself
how asks my daughter with kids
could he go out and do it
we're from different tribes a possible answer
even in love he moved like a bear
fox-eyes fox-tears fox-glove

Guess the luck ran out
guess the women got manhandled
guess he never quite made it to that
spirit inside him
all of us studying poisons
poison & rational inquiry & spirit
guess he brought a spirit mask
el tigré out of Oaxaca
then the abyss the long slope down
not a plummet when he
went from among us
a sinking

If the stream runs shallow
the water looks murky
give the book one superfluous word
it will not survive
people these days strive for   *Huai Shi*
surface effect trickery gimcrack
hold something back the poem
can go deep into history
if mountains stand high enough
earth ripples with *ling*

This here Jesus he was
a great doctor,
he had lots of power
I guess he was the best gambler in the United States
Myths & Texts the first place I saw it
back of that I heard
the señor of the brush tell it—
people need power for gambling
some might get women
find luck in the hunt, catch a song
everyone knows luck when they got it
it runs out & you're done

Look at shapes that got twisted
places the rock or soil
surged in curious ways
earth resisted the pressure of lava
granite thrust out of sandstone
Raga Todi's the mode of late morning   *105° longitude*
ice on Indian Peaks
we step through the watershed
rhythm music & time
on the map only Laramie & Prince Albert
have same sun-time as here

". . . it is necessary to visualize
their extremely intimate
contact with the trees
the rocks, the weather and the
delicate changes in the atmosphere,
with the shape of every
natural object, and, of course
with the habits not only of
every species of animal but of many
individuals."

Unroll the map—
luck is not far from the order of things
the whole length of the fortieth parallel
sunlight's consistent
South Arapaho Peak gets sun
same as Mendocino Bay   *40° latitude*
Boutou, Tashkent, Mt. Olympus
you cannot stress rational inquiry
then use a revolver like that
toyóú'uuwu, keep it in mind

At a certain point
you find you're no longer a seeker
you have a sense
what shape luck takes in your life
luck, power, the highest
energy back of the world
my friend sent the *Chanda Maharoshana*
Tantra with a note—
I give it only to people
over forty, & married

To have hold of some power
a gift of the animal world
niihénehéiзit
that's not how to say it
two petals up three lobes beneath
skullcap white bee balm
spicy oils make the body sweat
cleanse the blood
give hide & hair uncommon fragrance
such things occur freely in the
family of mint
before ritual binds it

Humans, mammals, birds, lizards
all semantically animate objects
sun moon the stars
the constellations too are animate
nouns for spirits, ghosts, the word cottonwood
some deer are just
common deer
others doctors and chiefs
lone autumn cry of the white tail
the power of grammar

In dream I am off to teach
in sub-Himalaya India
the book I need's missing
it's laden with spells, puzzles, & haiku
the rotating stars fool me again
Great Bear west ridge, Orion low to the south
pole star Wyoming
mountains cresting to Santa Fe
is the river a yellow line
if I speak this sort of riddle *koho'ówu'*
will blue lines
be tributary creeks

A mounting unease
can you safely use terms from
so many languages
I Ching says to stay modest, act with respect
the right foot gave out as I stepped
from the cabin
the carton of books strewn in the mud
have I broken my foot
broken trust with the unseen
sources of life

The thing about artifacts, tools, songs—
meddling is always a risk
how do you handle strange vowels
"I lifted a couple of
lines about Jon from the title poem
& slipped them into my own"
handle old words at times the way you'd
shy from a hoard of bones
testing the glottal stop
the syntax coils in its parfleche
how cool a distance
my friend keeps in his poetry

Back there away over
there in the past
a burial site
American dipper's an animate noun
nests in the waterfall, a sign the creek's
in good shape
could have gotten
flowers or incense, taken a song there,
police report the road he went out on,
cébtii, pass it along

Beaver lodge where the creek bends
green willows where we keep the stars
deep in Centaurus
gazing down
at the water dogs
N.O. Brown taught it as poetry
those paths that lead nowhere,
so build your lodge of
local material
ie. a longhouse

The right foot's broken in the
spirit world too
bright eyes where we keep the stars
she moves down the road
flanks of a panther
curled in each other's skin at night
painfully vulnerable
the acrid odor
graphics on her stretched skin
& sexual tinctures the *xo'éiyoo*

"Your friend's tea house
interests me as I am
about to embark on a project
to build a hut in the woods near here,
a retreat for a writer or artist or
green activist, taking its cue   *Pittenweem, Fife*
from early Celtic hermit poems—
to design & build
a contemporary version
of basic living."

Did you break your foot
did I hear that correctly
I was dozing off and somebody
told me or did I
dream it and what does it mean
= *my old mother* =
fur, hoofs, sticks, strings, bells
a considerable number of objects
are decorated
according to dreams

". . . and in part from their
development
of a LANGUAGE
that allows them to recognize
the place
and subsist in it
along with its other
animals, plants, spirits,
and geologic
forms."

Time now for *Raga Marwa*
early evening hour
North & South Arapaho peaks reddened
the plectrum avoids SA, the tonic
sundown over sierra
sharp edge shadow on tundra
his heart was torn from the afterlife   *Ali Akbar Khan*
I see the watershed's structure   *1922-2009*
hear its choked quiet notes
the old man's departed,
his medicine
gone back to clay

Lost in the raga's
ascending notes
the blue grove sets the mood
a dark-eyed junco flashes away
white tail feathers scissoring
one day you'll need a plant
a certain herb you've never met
step cautiously
if you bend its yellow florets aside
you open an abyss

Sundown comes
to everything animate
he stressed rational inquiry
then used his revolver
neh'etí
the bastards used oil as a decoy
we moved to protect the Arctic they went
into the vaults
education, retirement, the forests
they even drilled Detroit

The Malhars are played
to draw rain
this watershed moves like a raga
flint spear tips came off its glacier
intricate rhythms   *Mian ki Malhar*
I forget how to sing them
Mian Tansen sang and brought fire
but couldn't remember the rain notes
only his wife
could sing Malhar

Music that's linked to
earth's seasons
the life cycle of humans
marking moon's passage through heaven
life's as it plays through our bodies
upright pine posts
beams with green leafy boughs that
circle the dance ground at Taos
I shift my broken foot
the washtub bass comes to life

Down in Albuquerque
JB has refurbished a
saxophone from the '20s
I angle my foot on the bucket-bass
there are songs of the Arapaho drainage
before roads, gasoline, came out West
fork-tail swallow flashes over
the beaver pond
the saxophone, he calls it a conduit,
blue notes of the heart

A five finger-hole bone flute
a cave in Germany's hills
an open paw the stiff pads a hanging dewclaw
a griffon's leg bone or a "musical
tradition at the time modern humans   *35,000 B.P.*
colonized Europe"
we whistled to animals they
taught us good manners
here is an iPod here a large-breasted
nude figurine, a *fashionista*

Don Bartolomeo never
scolded, he never
said anything, he only looked
there are manners customs you don't
use a knife to pry with
you put tools back you don't interrupt—
very distant, way over there
outside this little camp you will be tested
you may search
but you cannot seize it

And the disjunction is
simply the way
we search for new images
your left breast I name horsetail
she has the power to heal ancestral wounds
the right breast's marsh marigold
pleasure & joy
each plant has a hydrological aspect
sun & soil crucial but how they use
water defines them

Find a drum that feels tranquil
find one of elk hide
get #23 wick at Ace Hardware
cut 4' plywood backing for bookshelves
study Arapaho grammar
practice singing buy garbage bags
your red hair spreads over the pillow
horsetail marsh marigold
I've seen those earrings before
scored on a
rock in New Mexico

Word came that you
shot yourself Jon
bark shreds young willows Land of the Dead
that day we climbed Bear Peak
I saw a bear amble like you
in Fern Canyon creek gully—
you thought studying coinage   *Jonathan Cohen*
& trade routes of coffee   *d. 5 May, 2007*
might bring a more equitable world—
tear the lid off the neoliberal jugglery—
Star path pilgrim old comrade take care
wherever you went the gift
circulated
that side-to-side gait
of the bear

If the slope gradient's steep
the water drains quickly
give the book too much emotion it
cannot survive
people these days muddy
the passions stir up froth on the surface
the poem that holds something back
can go far into history
if you study the ridgeline
you'll see earth ripple with *ling*

Animals & words combine
to fill the cabin
wet air from Utah brings thunder
tools weapons ceremonial items
whatever you find on the tundra
Arapaho Pass elk joints & grinding stones—
I lost what I had in Coeur d'Alene
once in a former life
and luck it appears, always cuts the
trail crosswise

He looked ragged in dress
was shabbily clad
dwelt in a state of spiritual poverty
hetebínouhúúni on earth it's little use
to pile up belongings
new clothes won't change your affairs
here in the spirit world you might
discover your human flesh gone
you'll be fashioned of
feathers & rawhide
wear turquoise
fear pride or courage go with you

Beneath the ill-fitting clothes
says *Isha Upanishad*
colorful beadwork won't help
tribal tattoos, piercings, don't get you far
what you do is perform works
hoping for a hundred
years life on earth
it's what you receive nothing else
medicines help but can't reach the deathless—
adds the sage darkly, there's no one
for karma to cling to

That's how it is
sinew & bone because a thing
isn't just used for
no reason
have you ever been lost in LA or London
our young people like
to wander strange cities
study customs listen to languages
can you find what makes
people laugh
no our young people they don't
just go off without reason
kookón

How has a mistake
shortcoming or misfortune enriched
your practice
the Buddhist magazine puts out the question
there are towns that get you in
trouble towns like Manali
Bhaktapur Bhubanesvar
I knew a woman in one who tattooed
her ankles claiming
she'd barter designs
for food in the afterlife

The black dog
got skunked
if you let him into the house
I'll be furious
oh doesn't it seem the mistakes
are all we can swap
in the afterlife
skunk stench in the hallway
black fur the white bathroom apologies
one hundred years of mistakes

Eagle cloud thundercloud
no frills or flounces
simple ten-line stanzas no word count
a ghost Robert says
is something that passes through
three generations
about how long it took
to hunt down the last Colorado wolf
some cope badly with trouble if
grandparents parents coped badly before them
70,000 wolf permits
issued in Idaho

Roads don't only
link points
heart, stomach, lungs, these
are for mountains
at top of this watershed stand the Arapahos
& the present road or something like it
was known to Paleo-Indians
game drive walls Folsom style spear points
people up here drive like they can't
get somewhere fast enough
as though roads
were only a nuisance

Solitude clear talk

no one seen

Nadia Liu rehearses the poem with gestures

moon pawlonia dangle yellow remorse

give me an eagle wand to inquire

where's the old man

gone says the boy the ravines

hills forests mist

gone looking for poisons

clouds too thick to see where

The thing about ghosts
& three generations is life's too short
to use garlic salt
Ronald Johnson has it that way
in his North America cookbook, *kookón*
you don't use a thing for just
any old reason
there is thunder and cancer
there are sisters-in-law
meals cooked at home & it is hard
to treat people with care

Who can say what a word is—
omen animal that knows the
winding spruce forest trails
gets through your head somehow
underground passways
filled with bright stolen corn
in China it's the great grey
rat-headed hamster
to emerge when the empire's in trouble
our empire's in trouble

Nadia gave me the Indian eagle plume
Red Pine the chukar-call
chukar or Eurasian partridge
considered a difficult hunt it
lives in high rock
I saw it at 14,000 feet in Ladakh
it feeds the old poets say
on moonbeams—
lay these items on the table
turn over the cards

"In the tracks
of animals or of stars
through the night sky"
how they scoured their own minds
for ways to help people
something about bone marrow
sap, semen, spirit juice a dead friend once
called it
the meaning of the broken foot?
could be Hilary's bone marrow cancer?
is the message hid in these stanzas
get tested as donor?

Water plants words
from these divination arose
key phrases burrow in thought
the great grey headed
rodent's warren of underground ways
when a nation's economy
crumbles the streets fill with
men holding *signs*
lost my job family willing to work
words plants water

When cats appear
there is omen
cougar at the bedroom window
silent taiga paw the shared
magnificence jaguars return to New Mexico
Pound knew the large felines presaged
"that nothing will happen"
what of Enron, Citgo, AIG
nothing that will be visible
to the sentries

The room I write in
its four directions
animalito masks to guard the creative life
ward off decay—
hey red-mouth Michoacan rat
narrow-headed turquoise coyote
keep the twin tyrannies from us
state & despotic religion the tarnished
mirror eyes of Guerrero el Tigré
overturn the room
assemblage of beasts

Thru a pitchpine wood
down a lower slope
inclosed by aspen
damp mist the beaver pond its
lodge four years empty night stars
I stand near *the origin of things*   *11 June 1851*
bass note, night hoofprints, elk wariness
the 21st century's *restless trivial* electronics
not what you look at, Thoreau
how you look & *whether*
you see

Roads don't only
link points
up here on foot buffalo-berry
bitter bitter under thick leaves
to be blown far from camp
tiny blueberry straw huckleberry
here where eagles control the thunder
the jagged 'Pawnee Forts'
overlook a drainage of scattered lakes the
trail provides gifts medicine-talk
places only
friendship can get

Death is not
coyote's fault
people ought to just go and
return he says,
four days answers hummingbird
four days the smell gets too awful
okay have it like that I'm going away
oh killing is easy, the Pomo basketmaker
observed, killing is easy it is
life that's hard to keep

Nééceenohoo
more gifts . . .
some offered in traditional
manner some the outcome
of a spontaneous heart
no foundation says *Diamond Sutra*
no motive as to the chukar-call Red Pine
weirdly handed me
the chukar partridge or Indian *chakora*
said to drink only moonlight
delicate passions they emerge in old poems
there go the nutcrackers
'pine birds'
flocking up-valley animate gifts

Only the rarest flavor
the purest melody
in Leadville stopping for gas
I went up the street for coffee
a few tourists on benches
early drinkers outside the bar
one shop features facsimile
gunfighter pistols
Wyatt Earp's motto, you have to
learn to be slow in a hurry

A good hunter
never lets anyone touch his tools
his bow his arrows his spear
thus our pens guarded
the notebooks & keyboards with masks
D.D. Kosambi says *vagura*
trap or snare
can refer to a writer
antler research is one path
her breasts are like birdsongs another

Standing near *the origin of things*
all creatures rocks trees
the moon the river
speak a common language
here you don't do things for just
any old reason
you respect things you don't break off
a branch you don't crush a leaf
even in dream her breasts
are two songs of one bird

Taking the owl's tooth
taking the six roads of changing & passing
beyond the far western pinnacles
it is dark to go back to the
notebook & read
the clues to a friend's suicide
WE'LL NEVER SOLVE THE RIDDLES
ALL IN ONE LIFETIME
not I said the fox
not I the wise woman

Girls shouldn't go
kicking around bear shit
jump over it taunt it
that's crazy behavior way past
the limits *hohóókee*—
a kind of crazy knowledge
lies out there
to find out the actual shape of
our lives the far high mountains
origins of poetry

No you don't just go out & talk
trash to a grizzly
the name 'bear' is already a ritual
distortion, the brown one
the sinewy one

With a heart like a clear spring
should you go to the edge of the berry patch
should you step over the rim
heart like clear water
kooh'úuwu'
the perilous weave of double this   *for Christine*
double that: *(is a poem*
for girls who play hand games)

September in Shadow Canyon
bear droppings plum pits
choke cherries the trail winds through
pines to Bear Peak young women
ample breasted making the climb
double double this
double double that
squawberry crabapple-seeds plum-pits
something tasting like lemon-grass
double this double that
black chokecherry red serviceberry
double double this that

"Even their
linguistic concepts seem to reflect
the nature of the land
they live in—"
hence Kroeber counseling Jaime
"put the letter about phonetics
into your revolver"
we are the people upriver
we stare at a 10,000 year tool cache
here in the land of the dead

What if you studied the tipi,
moccasins, parfleche, of people
who used to live around here
what if you jumped
over bear droppings out in the hills
"Grizzly has a huge anus!
"Bear makes a terrible husband!"
not to make mind into something
not to push mind out of the way
but to discover to re-
cover mind's actual shape

What if you are a writer,
do you jump over the dictionary
insult etymologies
go looking for trouble or
make fun of meanings
here's a world where knowledge brings trouble
words have a life of their own
each a tiny imagist poem
I blow across etymologies
like girls who jump over bearshit

Arapaho Traditions
Kroeber's #105 'the girl who became a bear'
C. Philip Rapid gave the account
Maria Johns a parallel
story between Weaverville & Whiskeytown
I smell gift exchange reciprocal
worlds along Route 299—
taunting draws a penalty
thoughtless words retribution
it's worse than a traffic offense—
crazy to let her wear claws
crazy to go out after her

They convey swift thought
across great distance
they do it with *po-o-kan-te*
how many friends rise or lumber bear-like
the proletariat a sleeping *arctos*
one old friend offers beadwork
he suggests the Western Diamondback
pattern as the rattlesnake shows
great care with boundaries
no, Dale, give me the Poison Path—
film of blindness no boundary

Circled Green Mountain
up Bear Canyon
guano on a tipped sandstone plate
Spanish from Quechua
falcon drips from the overhang
there are spirits you don't want
hanging around after death
an education in ecological balance
obscure tangled choices
burn head & tail no blame

Typically you see four toes
in the print
the metacarpal pads larger
than in canine tracks
shall I carry a revolver
the wind carries odor of gunpowder
courtyard mud holds the imprint
& learning how to track gives inference
that narrative is the specific
shape of your thinking
in this world your spine's straight
once the story is finished
when the story's told fully
your spine's
straight as bluestone

Out there curves a steep
geographic terrain
it links to the spirit world
you can sharpen your
teeth on coffee that's brewed there
even to whistle there's
a gesture that intensifies the *neséihi*—
the *wildness* where the tiny dry
fruit of the squawbush
puckers into a mask

I'm wondering what a lithium
mine does in the Chilean Andes
batteries for hybrid cars—
red hair sweeps across your face
that's one way to say it
he-enters-the-tent-lookingly
or enteringly-he-looks
our watershed sharpens with animal cries
when we enter they know it
they, the words themselves

Watched a coyote at dusk
slink one side a squawberry patch
seven mule deer
tails tucked, ears angled windward
nosing the snow
first one then another neck lifted
forelegs straight out
stepped towards the brush like dancers at Jemez—
should'a seen that dog run
dark pines up mesa *koo'óh*

Tells it to him makes
fun of him
I have pretty teeth & large breasts
took half of her tied to him he uncovered him
fractured his head gave him
medicine
"In short the undetermined, and to this writer's mind,
fundamental problem of Arapaho, Fox, and Algonkin
in general is whether these languages say 'he-enters-
looks,' 'he-enters-lookingly,' or 'enteringly-he-looks'"
night darkness beadwork,
grease cover hide

The foreman or perhaps owner
explained, unless we do this nobody
(he enters lookingly)
can bring their boats in here—
working their way down
the Doug fir & spruce slopes with chainsaws
the Chittendon slope
a seed pod void of seed
Nishikigi, the ghost work crew
stacking up batons
knotty pine for the nouveau riche

She continued speaking
the stories tangled into each other
raven dark wings by the fire
why do you recount the same stories
why night after night—
I am not, she said, doing it
for my own ears
the spirits tell me they've no
place to live
if you too would start singing
I won't have to repeat myself

On each Jemez dancer green fir sprigs
a young man in blue jeans
sprinkles white cornmeal
will the bankers get away with huge
bonuses the streets overflow
with out of work people
At Su K'wa K'e a flower
once blossomed
why today weep when I notice
that same yellow flower?
the rural districts hit hardest in some
every other house with a sign—
FOR SALE

Like wood, stone, ivory, or bone
it is a substance
full, old, rounded
soft as amber, enduring,
the next two songs are so
old we've forgotten
the words
inside them the black wing of a crow
no one can see
it but us

Word comes of Dilip
Chitre's death
who spent his life chiseling objects
from the poets of long-ago
Maharashtra
the ones who sang by the riverbank   *10 December 2009*
Muktabai so wild she ate
diamonds & said no, no
we Vakaris we do not hide out from life
we go out & face it
at eighteen a flash of purple lightning
she vanished, dear Dilip

These songs without talent
beneath their poisonous fonetiks
may they carry prayer
& good medicine
woxu' and *hówoo'óót*
our voices
our subtle human rhythms
can we be generous, cook for each other?
were we as the Haida say brought
from the soil for this purpose?
can we speak to animals
treat our young with respect?
it's true we throw fabulous parties

My father sat on a fallen trunk
rifle propped on his knee
upright the photograph torn leaving
the question what
or who sat beside him?
where's the missing half photo?
his mother's hand on the
verso *doesn't Tom look good*
could be Chile
California the Pacific Rim
family homeland could be Pearl Harbor
San Diego, Panama, the Phillipines
anywhere the navy
could reach

The Colt revolver,
the repeating rifle & windmill
along with barb'd wire
it's said these settled the West—
all else mere electronics built on old killings—
I remain partial to the indigenous bow
Latin *toxicum* poison
old Persian *taxsa* is arrow
no match for the Savings & Loan
Silverado the long line of our rip-offs

thanks to Joan Anderson

Armstrong Doolittle's Notched Diamond
Boone's Top-slot Visible Guard
Connelly's Knife-edge T-Bar
Devore's Wire Lock
Edenborn's Offset Barb
Gregg's Barbed Snake Wire
Harbaugh's Torn Ribbon
Mann's Semifluted Ribbon
Page's Half Hitch & Loop
Nadelhoffer's Flat-wire Gull Wing

Dilip your name means—
possibly, protector
question mark, of Delhi
down the page *diganta* is sky's end
rim of the horizon
The powder of pearls was thrown in the skies
how the eye sees the
comrade go smokes after death
cedar puffs white sage blue beads
perhaps remote once far distant
horizon's end more will we meet

My own one life a shape maybe
fashioned in Asiatic snares
the *vagura* has many spring-locks
barbed wire doesn't stretch far enough
to hold human affection—
poems grammar rough travel
raga brought to notable
ripeness by family military careers
(had not thought this before)
crossing the Pacific Rim
ancestral wounds are always geopolitical
threads of dark karma
Seattle where at the Navy memorial
for aunt Mary Anne
a priest pointed out the historic stained glass
backed by bullet-proof loxor

There's dream of Sushila
giving up her one year child
for adoption
Blake's Knee Grip she's had an abortion,
affair but I'm dream-shocked
Smith's Spool & Spurs
her husband would be more shocked—
to realize he's dead
thirty years armored entanglement
Merrill's Eight Point Coil with its barbs

As my family went,
west the slow shift underfoot
continents, reached the coast the
oaks scrubbed on hill slopes
towering redwoods or dry chaparral
the endless ranks of cars
up 101 or twist
inland where the one last lip
of habitable land, the edge
the edge is love the way you must find it

On the high Plains northwest
from Denver
the first nearly vertical
plates of the piedmont scored like two maps
two lives, Marlow,
is it the creek pressing down
archaic rock thrust into cliff's embrace
thou art a green plant to me
mint that makes
hair & hide fragrant
lance-shaped leaf by the creek

A smoke-blue tool cache
each scalloped edge
holds the scrapings of ghost horse & bear
recollect the loves the many
sorts of love, the predator lost track of,
the family members, women,
ghost grizzly ghost grey wolf
flaked edges I thought at Jemez after three
four hours the drum beat came
from the earth itself
flaked in the hooves of the buffalo

Is it a medicine lesson?

my daughter's turtle

burrows deep in the cedar chips

the turtle dream realm we know nothing of

Orion overhead a lesson in poisons?

the *wolf moon* lifts

it is gestures make up the verbs

a story picked into rock

horse, tree, bear, & now we long to share food

mud brought to surface under the

turtle legs

maybe mountains & creeks

or what could

the symbols mean

Black night without love
is a she-cobra
If the moon would rise I could
turn back the sting
But spells have proved futile
charms worthless—
now even love is extinguished
Without his dark love, Sur is a lost
snakebitten girl
convulsing with venom

piya binu nagini kari rat

Biologists on the plateau
studying wolf
incursions from Idaho
keep the name-taboo active—
'visitors from the north'
then photograph pawprints, send scat to the lab—
or where did you sleep last night
in the pines with the sinewy long-limbed one?
parda grammatica
her language in urine marks
Wolf did I know the lexicon
could read it off rocks with my nose
would you still prove *anamika*
name-less?

High Lonesome Ranch
DeBeque, Colorado

This watershed
the land itself is what survives
like a raga is sounded
can you see the curved way how it
rounds straight out ahead

Small twists in the rock a way forward
even love is *beebei'on,* call it
distant, way over there at
horizon's end,
to venture where love is most distant
science & storytelling at last

ON THE SONGBOOK

The poems "From the Arapaho Songbook" began to take shape in April 2009 out of efforts to learn Arapaho, a Native American tongue in the Algonkian language family. There are currently about 350 native speakers of Arapaho, some in Oklahoma, the majority in Wyoming where they share reservation land with the Eastern Shoshoni. Almost no Arapaho speakers live in Colorado these days, though this was traditional territory. The 1851 Treaty of Fort Laramie had given the Arapaho tribe land bounded to the north by the Wind River in Wyoming, to the south by the Arkansas River, and from the jagged pre-Cambrian rock pinnacles of the Continental Divide eastwards into Kansas.

I hoped excursions into Arapaho would disclose aspects of the Southern Rocky Mountain bioregion, where I live, that might otherwise go unnoticed. A bit of ecological training—learning to "read" the landscape—turned out to be instruction in linguistics. My concern was to get closer to plant, animal, rock, weather, or hydrological cycles, by way of the Native words that held them. The eco-zones & drainage systems here—which change quite fast due to the mountains' vertical pitch—

hold a wealth of geological & biological diversity. Under a heavy bolt of Spanish, French, and Anglo words a terrain of older speech.

It turns out that Andrew Cowell, a linguist at the University of Colorado, and Alfonso Moss, Senior, a native speaker from the Wind River Reservation, had recently published an important & quite serviceable grammar. Arapaho builds sentences by packing meaning into long, complex verbs—"the morphosyntax of the verb is the structural and conceptual heart of the language," writes Cowell. Much that European languages regard as noun or sentence, in Arapaho come forth as a single elegant verb.

Cowell I sought out since he lives nearby. The two of us have climbed the high country to the Continental Divide, talking linguistics & plant lore, poetics & place names. We have tasted dwarf blueberry, squawberry, the dry bitter buffalo-berry, and taken note of medicinal plants that people gathered for centuries. (In the tangle of modern geopolitics, these days it is mostly East & SE Asian immigrants who collect plants by the mountain creek-beds.) Our conversations, plus the re-workings Cowell & Moss have done of Arapaho songs recorded decades earlier, drew me into a whole other realm of poetry.

The songs I'm referring to had been collected, transcribed into Roman letters, translated into unpretentious English, and published in two sources. One is James Mooney's *The Ghost Dance Religion and the Sioux Outbreak of 1890* (1896). Mooney gives his opinion that of the tribes that produced ghost dance songs, "first in importance, for number, richness of reference, beauty of sentiment, and rhythm of language, are the songs of the Arapaho."

> *hohoot niiboot*
> *neniibéit-owoo*
>
> The cottonwood song
> I am singing it
>
> *Arapaho Ghost Dance, song #13*

The other collection is Frances Densmore's *Arapaho and Cheyenne Music*, published in 1936.

Cottonwoods line the creeks. They are structural hints to what Susan Howe calls the sleeping wilderness. Arapahoe is the name of the avenue that connects my home to my place of work. The asphalt heads west, past car dealers, Conoco pumps, groceries, directly towards a two-peaked ridge that looks like it hulks skywards where the pavement would end. I have been climbing those peaks since the 1970s. The Continental Divide runs along them. They were once called *hooxeihi-inenii beiinese'*, Pawnee trench. I have found no account of the skirmish that gave them the name. Thought of today as two separate peaks, North and South, they are spelt Arapaho, without the e.

NOTES ON THE POEMS

Protein residue occurs

In May, 2008, a cache of prehistoric tools was unearthed in Boulder, Colorado. The site lies about five minutes by automobile from Naropa University's campus, where I teach, in the yard of a fancy home tucked up towards the Ponderosa pine-covered foothills. The Mahaffey Cache—named for the Boulder resident and landowner whose gardener's spade sparked against the stone tools—contains eighty-three or eighty-four pieces of skillfully knapped stone. Somebody's, or some clan's, tool kit. From the hand-chipped butcher-tools scientists recovered 'protein residue' of the North American horse and camel—creatures that vanished under unknown circumstances about 13,000 years ago—and the American short-nosed bear.

What we call

Jaime de Angulo (1887-1950), American linguist, anthropologist, medical doctor, rancher, poet, novelist. Along the West Coast and through backwoods North America he is a legendary figure, largely based on a series of 100 broadcasts he did for KPFA radio, Berkeley, the year of his death. For a while a rumor circulated that a suitcase full of letters he'd written to his family in France was being burned. Along with excerpts from his writings, De Angulo shows up—a figure from an American Noh play —in some of these poems.

Two brilliant old cranks
Jaime de Angulo and Ezra Pound. They wrote back & forth the final year of de Angulo's life. Pound at the time was incarcerated at St. Elizabeth's Hospital ("bughouse") in Washington, D.C.

Ruth, why do you want
Ruth Benedict, American anthropologist. De Angulo wrote her after she'd appealed to him for an introduction to the Taos pueblo.

Dear Eck the word rut
Eck (Alec) Finlay, Scottish poet & artist. He maintains a keen interest in the Indian Peaks, and has drawn many poets into mountain range-based art & poetry projects. He keeps us alert to happenings in his local Schiehallion ranges.

If the stream runs shallow
Huai Shi, Chinese poet and calligrapher (ca. 7th century).

At a certain point
The Sanskrit *Chanda Maharoshana Tantra* is one of the strangest texts of Buddhism, set as a dialogue between Siva and his wife Parvati. It teaches the overcoming of personal likes and dislikes (which John Cage thought useless for the arts) through the most extreme sexual practices.

"Your friend's tea house
Letter from Scottish poet Thomas A. Clark.

The Malhars are played
Mian Tansen (ca. 16th century), court musician for India's Emperor Akbar, credited with giving shape to the Indian raga as we know it. The Malhars are a set of monsoon season ragas, based on a progression of notes that evoke (or regulate) rainfall. The particular version associated with Tansen is called Mian ki Malhar; oral tradition says his wife or lover invented it.

Don Bartolomeo never
See Jaime de Angulo's novella *Don Bartolomeo.*

Solitude clear talk
Tribute to a friend, Nadia Liu, who acts out the Chinese characters that make up classical poems. Several old poems enter this stanza in fragments, notably "Searching for the Master but not Finding Him" by Chia Tao (779-843).

The thing about ghosts
Ronald Johnson, American poet (1935-1998). Author of several cookbooks; the one referred to is *The American Table.*

Roads don't only
Pawnee Fort (*hooxeihiinenii beiinese'*) is the Arapaho term for North and South Arapaho Peaks. South Arapaho Peak, 13,347' elevation; North Arapaho, 13,502'.

Death is not
The Pomo Indian basketmaker is William Ranganal Benson (1862-1937). Benson became renowned for his traditional baskets, which

won first prize at the 1904 Saint Louis World's Fair. A close friend of Jaime de Angulo, together the two translated Benson's Pomo creation myth (*The Journal of American Folklore*, 1935).

Girls shouldn't go
Throughout North America the story of a girl who turned into a bear has been told. In some versions it is "The Woman Who Married a Bear." Fine versions by Sally Noble (Chimariko), Maria Johns (Tagish), and C. Philip Rapid (Arapaho) are available. Anthropologist Catharine McClellan collected eleven versions in the Pacific Northwest in the late nineteen-forties and early fifties.

No you don't just go out & talk
'Bear' means the brown one. Hunting cultures often observe a taboo against using the names of certain animals. They may use various diversionary terms: the old one, the brown one, the long sinewy one. Sometimes trophy parts also undergo distortion: racks instead of antlers. Ill-mannered humans call the animal by name, and on top of that insult him.

Typically you see four toes

Felis concolor. Mountain lion, cougar, panther, catamount, puma, painter—known by more names than any other North American mammal. Sightings are infrequent so it is worth knowing how to identify the paw print.

Word comes of Dilip

Dilip Chitre (1938-2009), Indian poet, painter, editor. He translated into English hundreds of songs by the *Vakaris* or medieval devotional poets of Maharashtra State, including Muktabai (b. 1279) who vanished at age eighteen in a purple lightning bolt.

Armstrong Doolittle's Notched Diamond

Names of patented barbed wires. Any history of the Western United States has to account for how much these changed the landscape. Frank Dobie (*The Coyote*) writes that when the strands appeared in Texas, sectioning the territory, no animal could cross it. Coyote spoke to the wire, eventually cutting a deal that allows him to slip through.

Black night without love

My translation of a song by Sur Das, blind singer of India (c. 1479-1584). The original occurs in Medieval Hindi. Typical of the *bhakti* tradition is for the poet to include his or her name in a signature-line, the *chap*, near the end of the song. *Piya binu nagini kari rat*: night without love is a [female] cobra.

Biologists on the plateau

Reports of possible wolf sightings on the High Lonesome Ranch in Western Colorado have wolf advocates intrigued & on edge. DNA tests are so far inconclusive. "Visitors from the north," used by the scientists & trackers, would be an example of taboo word substitution. Conservation biologists prove as superstitious as hunters or poets.

GLOSSARY

Note: all words are Arapaho except where otherwise indicated.

beebéí'on: far off, out there, away from camp

beiinese': trench, fox-hole, battlement, fort

cébtii-: to pass something along, hand it down

cé'eseitíít: diverse languages

cóoó: trap

dinihowii: (Achomawi or Pit River) medicine, spirit helper

heetééniihi': protect, take care of

heeteenoo3itoono: old time story

héétnoo3ítooné3en: I am going to tell you a story

hetebínouhúúni: pitiful, humble

ho'oowú: house

hohóókee: crazy person

hohóót: cottonwood

hooxéb: spring, mouth of a spring

hówoo'óót: prayer

ko'ootéíhi-: to be generous

koho'ówu: small stream

koo'óh: coyote

kooh'uuwu: clear water

kookón: for no reason

ling: (Chinese) life-force

nééceenóhóó: gift

neh'etí: to commit suicide

néíto'éíno': relatives, kin (plural)

neniibéit-owoo: I am singing it

neséihi: to be close to nature, wild

nih'óóʒoo: mythological trickster of the Arapaho;

also spider, white person

niibot: song

niihénehíʒit: to acquire some power or skill from a

supernatural source

niiinón: tepee

nooxóbé: frog

nótonohein: medicine, doctoring

núhu: here

pa-wi-ro-peku: (Proto-Indo-European) magical formula,
'protect men & cattle'

parda grammatica: (Latin) 'tawny grammar' (Thoreau)

po-o-kan-te: (Ute) spiritual power

tebiinis: broken horn

toyóú'uwuu: to hold or bear something in mind

vagura: (Sanskrit) trap or snare

wox: bear

woxu': medicine, spirit power

xo'éiyoo: salve, cream

yue 4: (Chinese) moon, month

Andrew Schelling lives in the Southern Rocky Mountains, dividing his time between Boulder, Colorado, and a former mining camp in the Indian Peaks. He has worked on land use in the American West, ecology, and wolf reintroduction. Recent books include *Old Tale Road* (poetry) and *Wild Form, Savage Grammar: Poetry, Ecology, Asia* (essays). For thirty years he has studied Sanskrit & Indian raga, and published seven books of translation from India's early poets, most recently a revised edition of *Dropping the Bow: Poems from Ancient India*. He teaches at Naropa University's Jack Kerouac School and at Deer Park Institute in India's bird-rich Himalayan foothills.

Photograph by Althea Rose Schelling

COLOPHON

Set in *Bulmer*.
William Bulmer was one of the fine printers of London.
In 1790, he took over the Shakespeare Printing Office and
incorporated as W. Bulmer & Co. He joined with the
punchcutter William Martin (1757–1830) and the partnership
helped elevate the quality of printing in England at the time.
The font which Martin designed retains an old face style while
experimenting with the contrast between thick and thin strokes.
Its color sparkles with balanced yet rhythmic beauty.

Book design by JB Bryan